GOLDEN RULES OF RELATIONSHIPS

Timeless Principles of Trust, Love, and Lasting Connections

KERRY LOTS

Dedication

"For those who value and cherish love, trust, and lasting connections in their relationships - may this book guide you in your journey of life."

Acknowledgment

I am deeply grateful to my parents for shaping me into who I am today, my teachers for the gift of education, and my friends, relatives and co-workers for teaching me the values of relationships.

Above all, to my family - thanks for letting me experience the deeper meaning of love, trust, and connection every day.

Disclaimer

The information contained in this book is based on the author's personal experiences and opinions. It is intended for general information and educational purposes only. It is not a substitute for professional advice, counselling, therapy or any form of expert consultation. While every effort has been made to ensure the accuracy and effectiveness of the information presented. The author and the publisher make no guarantees regarding the results obtained from following the recommendations described.

Readers are encouraged to seek professional advice when dealing with serious relationship issues or emotional challenges. The author and the publisher disclaim any liability, loss, or risk incurred as a consequence, directly or indirectly, of the use and application of any content in the book.

Preface

Relationships are the foundation of a fulfilling life. They bring meaning, joy, and a sense of belonging, yet they also require effort, patience, and understanding to truly flourish. Building and maintaining strong relationships is an ongoing process in our journey of life - one that demands attention, communication, and deep respect for the bonds we form.

This book explores timeless principles of trust, love and lasting connections to help you build and sustain meaningful connections in your life. These principles are not quick fixes or magic solutions; rather, they are enduring truths that can guide you through the wonderful, and sometimes challenging, path of relationships.

However, no book can offer a one-size-fits-all solution to every relationship challenge. Every bond is unique, shaped by individual experiences, personalities, and emotions. Instead of providing rigid answers, this book offers guiding principles to help you navigate relationships, with wisdom, flexibility, and care. It acknowledges the richness and complexity of human connection, encouraging you to approach your relationships with empathy, patience, and authenticity.

Within these pages, readers will find insights meant to inspire reflection and growth. Whether you are nurturing a new relationship, strengthening an existing bond, or healing from past wounds, the timeless lessons shared here are intended to serve as a compass on your journey.

May these insights inspire you to foster deeper, more meaningful, and lasting connections. May this also remind you that the true art of relationships lie in our daily choices to trust, to love, and to communicate with honesty and heart.

- **Kerry Lots**

Table of Content

Understanding the Core of Relationships

Relationships are like gardens - they require care, attention, and patience to thrive. Some flourish naturally, while others demand more effort. Yet, regardless of how they begin, meaningful relationships are built on certain timeless principles. Understanding these principles is the key to building stronger connections with the people who matter.

Every relationship begins with you. Before you can connect deeply with others, you must first know yourself. Your emotions, values, and past experiences shape how you respond to people and situations. If you've experienced betrayal, you may hesitate to trust. If you've faced rejection, you may struggle to open up. Recognising these patterns helps you see why you behaved the way you do - and where you may need to grow.

But trust and respect are not enough - understanding must follow. Understanding happens when you take time to see the world from the other person's perspective. It's listening not just to their words, but to the feelings behind them. Sometimes, understanding means stepping back from your own assumptions and asking : What is this person really trying to convey?

Communication ties all of these together. Many relationships falter not because people stop caring, but because they stop talking - or worse they start talking in hurtful ways. Expressing your feelings openly with honesty is crucial, but so is listening with patience. Instead of reacting impulsively during conflict, try pausing to reflect and take a second thought. Ask yourself : What am I really upset about? How can I explain this calmly? These moments of reflection can prevent minor misunderstandings from turning into lasting wounds.

Healthy relationships are built on balance - a fair exchange of giving and receiving. If one person gives endlessly while the other only takes, resentment grows. Acts of kindness, however small, nurture a sense of appreciation. Sometimes a thoughtful gesture; other times it's simply being present when someone needs you.

Of course, no relationship is without conflict. Disagreements are natura l- what matters is how you handle them. Anger often tempts us to lush out or withdraw, but true connection requires patience. Taking time to calm down, reflect, and then approach the issue with understanding can turn conflict into an opportunity for growth.

As time passes, relationships change. People evolve, priorities shift, and unexpected challenges arise. Relationships that survive are those that adapt. Embracing change rather than resisting it allows both to grow together. Above all, lasting relations are built on love-not just in words, but in actions. Love is shown through patience, forgiveness, and thoughtful gestures that say, I see you, I value you, and I'm here for you. Love isn't always easy but choosing to show it, even on difficult days, strengthens the bond you share.

Relationships are a journey - often filled with joys, challenges, and lessons. The more you nurture them with trust, respect, understanding, and love, the deeper and more meaningful they become. In the end, strong relationships aren't just about finding the right people - they are about being the right person, one who is waiting to give, listen, and grow.

INTRODUCTION

Why Trust, Love, and Connections matter

Trust, love, and connection are the cornerstones of every meaningful relationship. Each plays a unique role, yet they work together to create bonds that bring security, warmth, and belonging. Understanding how these elements function can help us build stronger relationships whether with our family, friends, or colleagues.

Trust is the foundation on which every strong relationship stands. Without it even love and connection can struggle to survive. Trust creates a sense of safety allowing people to be themselves without fear of judgment or betrayal.

In romantic relationships, trust allows partners to feel secure in each other's loyalty and intentions. It encourages openness - the freedom to express fears, dreams and insecurities without hesitation. A relationship rooted in trust gives partners the courage to be vulnerable knowing they will be accepted rather than criticized.

Between parents and children trust is essential for emotional stability. Children rely on their parents for guidance, protection and comfort. When parents keep their promises, provide consistent care and respond with patience instead of anger, children learn to trust. This trust shapes their confidence and willingness to share their thoughts openly. When parents break trust, by being overly harsh, unpredictable and dismissive - children may withdraw emotionally, creating distance that's difficult to mend.

Friendships thrive on trust as well. It allows friends to confide in one another, knowing their secrets are safe. In moments of hardship, trust reassures friends that they can count on each other. Without it, friendship risks becoming shallow, filled with doubt and hesitation.

Even in professional relationships, trust plays a vital role. Colleagues who trust one another collaborate more effectively, communicate openly, and share ideas without fear of judgments.

Trust creates a sense of reliability, ensuring that tasks are handled with honesty and accountability. In workplaces where trust is lacking, tension builds and teamwork suffers.

While trust forms the foundation, love builds life into relationships. Love is more than just emotion: it's an ongoing choice to care, support and nurture.

In romantic relationships, love reveals itself through affection, understanding and shared experiences. It's found in simple gestures - a warm smile, a comforting word, or a thoughtful act. When couples actively express love, they create an emotional bond that strengthens their connection.

Between parents and children, love is protective and unconditional. It's a force that reassures a child they are valued, even when they make mistakes. A loving environment allows children to explore, learn, and grow without fear of rejection. Simple actions - like listening attentively, offering praise,or sharing meaningful moments - reinforce these bonds. When children feel loved, they develop confidence and a strong sense of self.

Love is equally important in friendships. While it may not carry the same intensity as romantic love, it thrives in loyalty, kindness, and encouragement. A loving friend offers support during tough times, celebrates successes and shows patience during moments of conflict.

Even in professional settings love - expressed through respect, compassion, and empathy - creates a positive environment. It's shown when colleagues show kindness, offer help, or acknowledge each other's efforts. Though subtle, this form of love strengthens workplace relationships and promotes teamwork.

Connection is what keeps these relationships alive and meaningful. While trust provides security and love nurtures warmth, connection is the energy that binds people together.

In romantic relationships, connection deepens when couples spend time together, engage in meaningful conversations and create shared memories. Connection builds intimacy - a sense that both people truly know and understand each other.

For parents and children, connection is formed through simple yet powerful moments - reading bedtime stories, playing games, or having heartfelt conversations. These interactions create lasting memories and provide children with a sense of belonging. Parents who prioritize connection build stronger bonds with their children ensuring they feel heard, valued, and supported.

Friendships also require connection to thrive. Staying in touch, sharing experiences and being present during important moments keeps friendships strong. A connected friendship provides comfort during hardships and multiplies joy during celebrations.

In the workplace, connection builds cooperation and trust. Colleagues who connect on a personal level- even through casual conversations or shared experiences - communicate better and work more effectively as a team. The sense of connection fosters a positive environment where people feel valued and motivated.

Trust, love, and connection are distinct yet deeply intertwined. Trust creates the security to be open, love nurtures emotional warmth, and connection keeps those bonds alive. When all three are present, relationships become strong enough to endure challenges, misunderstanding, and change. However, when one element is missing, relationships can weaken. Without trust, doubt creeps in. Without love, warmth fades. Without connection, even the most stable bond can become distant.

Whether in romance, family, friendship, or professional life, embracing these principles leads to deeper relationships, stronger support systems, and a greater sense of fulfillment. The effort to build trust, express love, and maintain connection is the key to relationships that last and bring lasting joy.

CHAPTER 1

The Art of Building Trust

"Have you ever wondered why some relationships thrive while others crumble under the weight of doubt and uncertainty?"

"What is the invisible force that binds people together making them feel secure, valued and understood?"

Why trust is the cornerstone

Trust is the foundation of every meaningful relationship, whether personal or professional. It fosters a sense of safety, allowing individuals to open their hearts without fear of betrayal. When there is trust, people feel valued, heard and respected, creating an environment where true connection can flourish. Trust strengthens bonds by fostering honesty, loyalty, and a willingness to be vulnerable.

Without it, even the strongest relationships can falter under the weight of doubt, suspicion, and miscommunication. Consistency, transparency, and reliability are key elements that sustain trust over time. When your actions align with your words, people will learn that they can depend on you.Trust is not built overnight; it grows steadily through small, everyday actions that demonstrate care, integrity, and accountability. It is the invisible thread that ties relationships together, making it essential for building lasting love, deep friendship, strong partnerships and meaningful communities.

Honesty Without Harshness

Honesty without harshness involves expressing the truth with empathy and respect. For example, instead of saying, "Your presentation was boring," you could say, "I think adding some visuals might make your presentation more engaging." Similarly, rather than criticizing a friend with "You always cancel plans," you might say, "I miss spending time with you ; let's plan something soon." This approach promotes openness while preserving relationships, making feedback easier to accept and act upon.

Being honest is essential for building strong relationships, but how we express honesty matters just as much as the truth itself. Speaking the truth with kindness creates space for openness without causing unnecessary hurt. It allows honesty to be a bridge instead of a barrier.

When addressing sensitive issues, focus on facts. Even if you are certain of the truth, avoid attacking or blaming the other person. Gentleness in your words and tone can make a significant difference in how your message is intercepted. It shows that your intention is to help, not to hurt.

Choosing appropriate, constructive words is key. Instead of pointing out someone's flaws harshly, express your thoughts in a way that encourages growth. Using language that uplifts while attempting correction fosters positive change.

Being direct is important, but it should be paired with a calm and steady tone. Clear communication eliminates confusion, and a gentle delivery ensures that honesty does not feel like an assault. People are more receptive and open to truth if it is conveyed with gentleness and care.

Finally, staying humble about your own imperfections keeps your honesty alive. Recognizing that everyone, including yourself, is imperfect brings a sense of shared humanity to your own words and actions, making honesty a gift rather than a weapon.

Consistency: The Silent Pillar of Trust

Being consistent in a relationship requires conscious effort. It's about showing up daily - not with grand gestures, but with small dependable actions that communicate, "You can count on me." In the beginning people may not notice everything you do. But, overtime, your steady and consistent actions will speak louder than words, and your commitment will not go unnoticed.

True consistency doesn't beg for applause or praise. You don't need to highlight every good deed or remind people of all the times you were there with them. Just keep doing what's right. Resist the urge to seek constant validation; real love doesn't demand recognition at every turn. Seeking appreciation for every act can appear childish and immature. Instead, find satisfaction in your own identity.

People observe more than they express. They feel with their hearts and reflect in their own time. Even if your efforts seem invisible now, they are registering at a deeper level. Consistency builds a quiet confidence in others - they start to trust you not because you promise, but because you live up to it every time.

There may be moments when you fall short, but don't be disheartened. What matters most is your will power to keep going. Get back up, re-commit, and continue showing up. Consistency doesn't mean perfection - it means persistence. Be reliable, not stagnant, in course to time, you'll realize that these silent pillars are the foundation on which trust is built.

Overcoming Betrayal and Rebuilding Trust

Betrayal shakes the very foundation of a relationship, leaving pain, doubt, and uncertainty. Rebuilding trust is not easy, but it can be possible with effort, patience and a willingness to heal. Open communication is the key - acknowledging the hurt and understanding why the betrayal occurred. Both parties must be honest about their feelings and intentions so that they can move forward,

Forgiveness is a choice, not a one-time event. It requires time and commitment. The person who broke the trust must be ready to take responsibility and consistently demonstrate reliability, transparency and sincerity. Trust is not restored overnight; it grows gradually through small, meaningful actions.

For the betrayed partner, learning to trust again means letting go of fear and resentment. It involves focusing on the present and recognizing genuine efforts rather than constantly revisiting the past. However, boundaries should be established to prevent repeated mistakes.

Once trust is rebuilt, it is important to nurture it. Avoiding bringing up past betrayals after they have been resolved, as doing so can reopen wounds and hinder progress. Instead, focus on strengthening the bond through love, respect and shared experiences. A relationship that overcomes can emerge even more resilient and deeply connected than before.

CHAPTER 2

Communication: the Heartbeat of Relationships

"How often do we truly listen to understand rather than just to respond?"

"Isn't communication more than just words-expressed through silence, gestures, and even the emotions we leave unspoken?"

Listening with Intent

Listening with intent is more than just hearing words; it's about being fully present and engaged in the conversation. It requires focus, patience, and an open mind. When we listen with intent, we tune in not only to what is said but also the emotion behind the words. This creates a safe space where the speaker feels valued and understood.

Intentional listening means resisting the urge to interrupt or mentally prepare a response while the other person is speaking. Instead, it involves maintaining eye contact, offering an affirming gesture and responding thoughtfully. In relationships, this form of listening builds trust, strengthens emotional bonds, and reduces misunderstandings. It encourages deeper conversations, allowing people to share their true feelings without fear of judgment. By listening with intent, we show empathy, foster connection and create meaningful dialogue. Ultimately, those who listen with care become the people others turn to in times of need.

The Role of Non-Verbal Communication

Non-Verbal communication plays a vital role in building and nurturing relationships. Often action speaks louder than words. A warm smile can brighten someone's day, while steady eye contact shows sincerity, attentiveness, and emotional presence. Simply holding someone's gaze with warmth and patience can make them feel seen, heard, and valued. Silence, too, speaks volumes. Sitting quietly beside someone during tough times, without rushing to offer advice or solutions, can be more comforting than words.

Beyond gestures, our daily actions-through our work, manners, character, and attitude-consistently communicate who we are and what we value. Reliability, respectfulness, and kindness shown in our everyday behavior build strong foundations of trust.Small thoughtful gestures, like adjusting a partner's scarf on a cold day, arranging a bed neatly, or serving a comfortable meal after a long day's work, silently express love, consideration and understanding.

Non-verbal cues are often most powerful when they are simple and spontaneous. Offering a favourite snack without being asked, holding the door open, a gentle touch on the hand during a stressful moment - all these show emotional availability and empathy. Even the way we listen - nodding slightly, maintaining an open posture, refraining from distractions - strengthens the connection without uttering a word.

Manners and character, too, are daily forms of silent communication. A respectful tone, genuine courtesy, and patience towards others reflect deep-seated values. Our attitude - whether it's one of gratitude, positivity, or compassion - can influence the emotional climate of our relationships more than elaborate speeches ever could.

In essence, thoughtful non-verbal actions communicate emotions words sometimes fail to capture. They offer quiet reassurance, deepen trust, and nurture bonds in ways that verbal communication alone cannot. When practiced with sincerity, these simple habits of care enrich relationships at every stage.

Navigating Difficult Conversations.

Navigating difficult conversations requires patience, empathy, and a clear focus on resolution rather than confrontation. Begin by approaching the situation with an open mind, ensuring you're calm and composed. Taking the lead to start the conversation demonstrates courage and a willingness to address the issue, which can set a positive tone. Avoid being defensive ; instead, listen actively and give the other person space to express their thoughts without interruption. Acknowledge your role in the situation, admitting your fault if necessary, as this shows accountability and encourages the other person to respond similarly. Refrain from casting aspersions or excessively pointing fingers, as blame only fuels tension. Instead, focus on understanding the other person's perspective validating their feelings. Using "I" statements rather than "you" accusations can help frame concerns without sounding confrontational. Maintain a calm and respectful tone throughout, and strive for clarity in your words to avoid misunderstandings. Be patient, as some conversations may take time to reach a resolution. Ultimately, the goal should be to find common ground, foster understanding, and strengthen the relationship rather than "win" the argument.

CHAPTER 3
Defining Love

"Is love just a fleeting emotion, or is it the foundation that holds relationships together beyond romance?

Can true love exist without a balance of passion, affection, and deep respect?"

Essence of Love

Love is more than a fleeting emotion; it is a conscious choice reflected on how we treat others. True love is slow to anger, it does not react impulsively, it responds with patience and understanding. When frustrations arise, love pauses, reflects, and chooses calmness over conflict. Being slow to anger does not mean ignoring problems but addressing them with wisdom and empathy.

Love endures through challenges, disappointments, and even moments of doubt, it never fails. While emotions may waver, love anchored in commitment remains steadfast. It is not measured by grand gestures alone but by consistent acts of care, support, and loyalty. True love preserves, finding strength even in difficult times.

Unselfish love puts the well-being of others above personal gain. It does not demand attention or repayment but gives freely. In unselfish love, small acts of kindness often speak louder than words. Listening without judgment, offering help unconditionally,without hesitation, and choosing compassion over pride reflect a love that nurtures and sustains.

Forgiveness is an essential part of love. Relationships are bound to face misunderstandings, hurt, or disappointment. Yet love chooses to forgive - not a sign of cowardice or weakness, but as an act of courage and strength. Forgiveness does not erase the past, but it creates space for healing and restoration. By letting go of resentment, love thrives on trust, peace and renewed connection.

Love, in its truest form, is patient, enduring, selfless, and forgiving. It weathers storms and celebrates victories. It is not perfect, but it is persistent - choosing understanding over anger, commitment over convenience, and grace over bitterness. Love grows stronger when nurtured with intention, and its impact leaves a lasting imprint on the heart it touches.

Love Above Romance

True love transcends fleeting moments of passion. It thrives in the quiet, consistent acts of care and strengthens bonds. A thoughtful gesture, a kind word, or simply being present can leave a lasting impact. Love isn't always grand ; sometimes it's found in the smallest sacrifices - a warm meal prepared after a long day, a comforting touch in times of distress, or a listening ear when words feel heavy. These simple acts never go unpaid, they blossom over time, deepening trust and nurturing connection. In love what matters most isn't the size of the gesture but the sincerity behind it.

Sometimes what feels like love in youth is more of an infatuation - a strong rush of emotions without a deep understanding or commitment. Real love, however, matures with time and is proven through consistent actions. A person who cannot love deeply may still engage in romance - grand dates, sweet messages, extravagant gestures - but without the willingness to sacrifice, forgive, or stay when times get hard, such romance fades quickly. Genuine love shows up in everyday life: in choosing patience during disagreements, standing by someone during an illness, or helping them pursue their dreams without jealousy.

For example, romance may be bringing flowers on a special day, but love is showing up to support someone during their worst days without being asked. Romance is whispering sweet promises: love is keeping them even when no one is watching. A partner who genuinely loves will not only enjoy the high points but also carry some of the weight during the low points. True love strengthens itself with actions, not just emotions. Real love is revealed in how someone stands by you during life's tough challenges.

Balancing Passion, Affection and Respect

Balancing passion, affection and respect is key to building strong and lasting relationships. Embrace your feelings with moderation - express your emotions without overwhelming the other person. Show genuine enthusiasm when sharing experiences, but ensure your excitement leaves room for their thoughts and feelings.

Demonstrate care consistently, not just during moments of joy or hardships, but in everyday interactions. Small gestures of kindness, attentiveness, and emotional support can reinforce the strength of any relationship.

Respect is the foundation that holds it all together - listen actively, value their opinions, and honor their boundaries. By blending these elements thoughtfully, you create a bond that nurtures connection, builds trust, and strengthens your relationship over time. Respect also involves allowing personal space, respecting individuality, and encouraging personal growth within the relationship.

Balancing them together requires mindfulness and intentionality. It is easy to be swept away by passion or to take affection for granted, but maintaining a conscious effort to respect, appreciate, and understand each other creates a deeper, more resilient relationship. When these elements are woven together with care, relationships become sanctuaries of love, resilience, mutual empowerment, capable of weathering all seasons of life.

The Power of Unconditional Love

Unconditional love forms the heart of every lasting relationship. It is about loving through thick and thin, without setting conditions based on mood, mistakes, or convenience. True love is consistent, not something you offer only when life feels easy, or when you are getting what you want. Imagine a partner who stands by you everyday, but you show them affection only when it suits you - such a love would feel hollow. Genuine love shows up even when it's difficult.

Mistakes, too, are part of being human. If your loved ones slips or fall short, it doesn't mean you withdraw your love. I remember when a close friend missed an important event in my life. Instead of taking it personally, I reminded myself that our years of friendship weren't defined by one forgotten moment. Real love forgives and continues, stronger for the understanding it shows. Another important aspect is loving without expecting anything in return. When love is tied to rewards or recognition, it becomes a transaction rather than a gift. True love is freely given, simply because it's who you are - not because of what you hope to get.

Moreover, while it's natural to love your family more deeply, the circle of your love should not stop there. The world needs more kindness and warmth. A smile for a stranger, patience for a coworker, or understanding for a difficult neighbour are all acts of unconditional love that ripple far beyond what we see.

Most importantly, love should flow naturally from the heart, not be performed out of obligation. Love given out of duty feels cold and mechanical. If your heart isn't in it, it's better to pause and reflect. True love is a living, breathing force - something you choose to give, with joy and sincerity, every single day.

CHAPTER 4

The Role of Empathy and Understanding

"Can we truly connect with others if we never try to see the world through their eyes?"

"Isn't empathy-not just agreement-that strengthens relationships and helps us navigate differences with compassion?"

Walking in their Shoes

Understanding others requires more than observing their actions - or demands empathy. Before forming conclusions, pause and reflect on their circumstances. Imagine their struggles, pressures and emotions. Ask yourself: What burdens might they be carrying rather than reacting impulsively, choose curiosity over judgment. For instance, if a colleague seems withdrawn or irritable, they may be battling overwhelming deadlines, workplace pressure, or personal struggles. Instead of assuming indifference or hostility, consider approaching them with kindness. A simple gesture - like asking, "Hey, is everything okay?" or offering to help with a task - can break tension and show you really care. Sometimes, people just need to feel seen and supported.

Engage in thoughtful conversations, ask questions, and listen with intent. By creating space for honest dialogue, you replace assumptions with understanding. Addressing concerns constructively not only eases tensions but also strengthens trust. Empathy creates a sense of emotional safety, where people feel valued and understood. Walking in someone's shoes isn't just about understanding their struggles ; it's a conscious effort to nurture deeper connections and lasting relationships.

How Empathy Builds Stronger Connections.

Empathy is the invisible bridge that brings two hearts closer. Rooted deeply in many religious teachings and reflected across centuries of literature, empathy has always been seen as essential for building real, lasting bonds. From ancient scriptures to modern novels, the message is clear: understanding another's feelings is the heart of human connection.

While sympathy is valuable, it is not the same as empathy. Sympathy is standing beside someone, feeling sorry for their pain, but often from a distance. You recognize their struggle, but you remain outside of it. Empathy, however, invites you to step inside their world. It asks you to feel with them - to suffer when they suffer, to rejoice when they rejoice.

For instance, a friend once shared how overwhelmed he felt balancing work and family. Offering sympathy I might have simply said, "That must be hard," and moved on. But practicing empathy meant something more - I sat with him, and for a moment, tried to feel the pressure he was carrying. I didn't rush to offer advice or solutions. I stayed with him in that space. That simple act made him feel seen, not just heard. It strengthened our friendship in ways words alone never could.

In daily life, we often blur the line between sympathy and empathy without realizing it. A colleague grieving a loss doesn't need just a polite "I'm sorry for your loss." They need someone who sits quietly with them during lunch, someone who acknowledges their pain without trying to fix it or move past it too quickly.

Empathy is a choice which requires effort, patience, and willingness to be vulnerable yourself. Next time you interact with someone struggling - or celebrating - pause and step into their shoes. Feel their emotions as your own. When you do, you build not just conversations, but lasting, meaningful relationships rooted in trust and love.

Developing Emotional Intelligence in Relationships.

Emotional Intelligence is the ability to recognize, understand, manage, and influence emotions - both your own and those of others. It encompasses key components such as self-awareness, self-regulation, motivation, empathy, and social skills. In the context of relationships, Emotional Intelligence becomes a powerful tool for creating deeper connections, resolving, and fostering trust.

Emotional Intelligence plays a vital role in nurturing relationships within families, friends, and workplaces. Self-awareness is key - understanding your emotions helps you manage them effectively. Controlling emotions during tense moments allows for calmer responses, preventing conflicts from escalating.

Empathy strengthens this process by helping you understand others' feelings, fostering trust and deeper connections. Active listening is equally crucial, as it encourages open communication and minimizes misunderstandings. Emotionally intelligent individuals also adapt well to social situations, offering support and encouragement where needed.

By combining self-awareness, emotional control, empathy and active listening, people can build stronger relationships and create positive environments wherever they connect.

Developing Emotional Intelligence also enhances conflict resolution skills. Instead of reacting impulsively, emotionally intelligent individuals approach disagreements with understanding and a willingness to find common ground. They are better equipped to validate others' feelings while maintaining their own boundaries respectfully.

Furthermore, EI contributes to resilience in relationships. It helps individuals bounce back from setbacks, views challenges objectively, and maintain a solution-focused mindset.

Practicing EI daily- through reflection, mindful communication, and emotional regulation-can transform interactions, making relationships more authentic, compassionate, and fulfilling over time.

Navigating Differences with Compassion

Navigating differences with compassion begins with embracing empathy - the ability to step into someone else's shoes and see the world from their perspective. Empathy isn't just about feeling sorry for others;it's about connecting with their struggles and offering understanding.

Mercy plays a crucial role in this. When someone wrongs you - even deeply - forgiveness can break the cycle of bitterness. I recall a friend who was betrayed by a close relative in a financial matter. Though hurt, he chose forgiveness over resentment. By letting go, he found peace and preserved the relationship. Forgiveness doesn't excuse the wrong ; it frees you from carrying the burden of anger.

Sympathy is equally powerful. Loving others as you love yourself means treating them with the same respect and kindness you hope to receive. A simple act of listening can ease someone's pain. Once, I noticed a colleague withdrawing from conversations. Instead of ignoring it, I reached out. Over coffee he opened up about personal struggles, and that moment of connection lifted his spirits

Compassion demands action. Whether it's offering support to someone in distress or helping a neighbour without expecting gratitude, selfless acts leave lasting impressions. When you extend a helping hand without seeking recognition, you inspire others to do the same.

True compassion reveals itself in actions more than words. By showing understanding in moments of conflict, you create bridges where walls once stood. In a world divided by differences, empathy is the thread that weaves people together.

CHAPTER 5

Boundaries and Personal Space

"Can a relationship truly thrive if personal space and individuality are constantly overlooked?"

"Isn't setting healthy boundaries the key to maintaining both closeness and self respect?"

Why Healthy Boundaries Matter

Healthy boundaries are essential for emotional well-being, positive relationships, and personal growth. They help individuals protect their mental, emotional, and physical space while fostering respect and understanding in interactions.

Establishing emotional space allows you to separate feelings from those of others, preventing emotional overload. Boundaries also protect your identity reinforcing your values, beliefs, and individuality.

This protection ensures you to stay true to yourself without feeling pressured to conform.

Independence thrives when boundaries are respected. Having personal space gives you the freedom to think, decide and act without constant influence. It encourages self-reliance and builds confidence. Quiet time is equally vital, offering moments of stillness to reset your mind, enhance creativity and reduce stress. Taking time to reflect allows you to process emotions, evaluate goals, and make thoughtful decisions. Privacy, whether emotional, physical, or digital is crucial for maintaining trust and ensuring everyone feels safe and respected.

Healthy boundaries also empowers you to express your rights and feelings without fear of judgment. This open communication strengthens relationships and encourages mutual respect. Boundaries are a sign of trust - they demonstrate that you value your own limits and are willing to honor those of others.

Lastly, learning to sayno is key to preserving your well-being. Declining requests that conflict with your priorities or overwhelm you is not selfish - it's essential for maintaining balance. By setting clear boundaries, you create a space where respect, self-care and healthy connections can flourish.

Boundaries and Personal Space

Learning to say NO without guilt is essential to protect your personal space and maintain emotional balance. Setting boundaries allows you to prioritize your well-being while staying true to your values.

When expressing your viewpoint or making a decision, be clear and direct. Avoid hesitation or excessive explanation. For example, say: "I understand your viewpoint, but I can't change my decision as I believe it's the right thing to do."

Providing a reason for your stance can help others understand your position. Be concise yet firm. For example, "I'm unable to attend because I've already committed to some personal time."

When your goals, values, or well-being are at stake, holding your ground becomes essential. While some may initially criticize you for being rigid, they are likely to respect your honesty and conviction in the long run.

Effective communication plays a significant role in reinforcing your point. Use a calm but assertive tone, maintain eye contact, and speak with confidence. This ensures that even if others perceive your point as harsh or direct, they will understand that your decision is reasonable and fair.

Remember, saying NO is not selfish;it's an act of self-respect. Prioritizing your well-being isn't just important - it's necessary for leading a balanced and fulfilled life.

Creating Space for Growth and Independence

Creating personal space is good for nurturing growth, fostering independence, and maintaining mental clarity. While relationships thrive on connection, carving out your own space allows you to develop a strong sense of self. Establishing boundaries is not an act of selfishness or arrogance - it's a mark of self-respect and balance.

When you take control of your schedule, prioritizing your own tasks without excessive influence from others, you send a clear message that your time and choices matter. Adjusting your plans occasionally to accommodate others is thoughtful, but sacrificing your priorities consistently can lead to frustration and burnout.

Setting boundaries isn't about shutting people out; it's about creating room to grow within.

By protecting your personal space, you create an environment of self-reflection, learning, and creativity. This intentional separation is what reflects character, purifies thoughts, and reveals your true potential. Many great thinkers and innovators thrived because they valued solitude as a space for growth and discovery.

When you manage your time intentionally, you take control of your life direction.

When you are undisturbed by constant demands or external pressure, you unlock the freedom to explore your thoughts, reflect on your experiences, and make meaningful decisions. Personal space fosters inner calm, boosting emotional stability and resilience.

Taking ownership of your time, actions, and choices is empowering. By doing so, you build accountability and cultivate a sense of independence that strengthens your identity.

Independence flourishes when you embrace solitude as a platform for self- discovery.

Embracing personal space is not isolation - it's an investment in your emotional well-being and long-term fulfillment.

Balancing Togetherness and Individuality

Each of us is unique, with our own likes and dislikes. Our preferences and inclinations cannot be taken for granted, especially in relationships. Boundaries, often misunderstood as barriers, should not be seen as negative when applied in a healthy relationship. Instead, they are essential for maintaining respect, understanding, and emotional well-being.

However, setting personal boundaries is important, it must be done with care. An extreme focus on individuality can strain relationships, creating emotional distance and disconnection. This is why balance is key - striking a middle ground between honoring personal space and fostering shared experiences.

In relationships boundaries are not walls; they are bridges that connect individuals while preserving their identity.

In the busyness of life, it's easy to become too engrossed in our own activities, unintentionally neglecting our relationships. Over time, this neglect can create a vacuum that widens the emotional gap - one that may be difficult to mend. Nurturing relationships requires intentional support.

Neglecting a relationship for too long can create a void that's harder to fill than we often realize.

Supporting and encouraging one another is vital. While it's natural to depend on our partner for comfort and strength, cultivating self-reliance is equally important.

A healthy relationship thrives when both partners strike a balance between togetherness and personal growth.

Ultimately, maintaining a strong relationship is about respecting boundaries, nurturing personal growth, and creating meaningful connections through shared goals. By embracing this balance, we foster relationships that are both fulfilling and enduring.

CHAPTER 6

Conflict Resolution for Stronger Bonds

"Is conflict a sign of a falling relationship, or can it be a doorway to deeper understanding and growth?

Isn't it true that resolving disagreements with patience and forgiveness strengthens bonds rather than breaking them?"

Turning Arguments into Opportunities

We are not machines; we are human beings. Arguments are natural, and they can even be healthy if handled constructively. Instead of feeling guilty for arguing, we can see it as an opportunity to clear misunderstandings, express concerns, and strengthen our relationships.

The key lies in how we argue. Controlling raw emotions during heated moments is crucial. Anger often pushes us to say things we later regret. Instead, pause and take a moment to calm yourself. A brief pause can make a huge difference. Emotions are powerful, but self-control is stronger.

Sometimes, seemingly minor mistakes can cause major damage if we let frustration take over. Practicing patience, responding thoughtfully, and giving yourself a second thought before speaking can prevent irreversible harm. Afterward, you'll feel satisfied knowing you handled the situation with maturity. Patience in conflict often leads to peace in relationships.

Mistakes are a part of our life, and they can be good if viewed positively, they help us understand our weaknesses, understand our limitations and grow from them. Instead of seeing mistakes as failures, we can use them as opportunities for self-reflection and improvement, ultimately strengthening our relationships and communication.

Arguments can actually set things right if approached with the right mindset. The key is to ignore your ego. Rather than focussing on proving a point, aim to understand and resolve the issue. Be an active listener, even when you feel frustrated. Listening shows respect and creates space for better understanding. Listening isn't about hearing words; it's about understanding feelings.

Avoid panicking or losing control during heated moments ; doing so often leads to regret. Before reacting, ask yourself: Am I arguing to fix something or to win the argument? This question can shift your focus toward resolution rather than confrontation.

Refrain from fault-finding. Instead of dwelling on what the other person did wrong, focus on what you can do to improve the situation. Having the courage to admit your mistakes fosters trust and mutual respect.

Conflict isn't the enemy - unresolved issues are. When you embrace arguments as opportunities for growth, you turn tension into deeper trust and stronger bonds.

Effective Conflict Management Strategies

Conflict is an inevitable part of relationships, but how we manage it can either strengthen or weaken our bonds. Understanding the root cause is crucial. Often, the real issues lie deeper than what appears on the surface. Uncover the roots before addressing the branches. Hidden frustrations, unresolved past grievances, or unspoken concerns may trigger present conflicts. Taking time to reflect and address these underlying issues can also prevent the present conflict and future misunderstandings.

Next, adopt a mindset of compromise. One hand alone cannot create a handshake. Effective conflict resolution requires both parties to participate. Finding middle ground where both individuals feel heard and valued encourages cooperation.

It is also important to recognize that pride can prevent us from admitting fault. No one wants to lose, even when they know they're wrong. Instead of focussing on who's right, strive to achieve a solution where both parties can share responsibility. Taking ownership together - whether equally or based on fair judgment - builds mutual respect.

Avoid the temptation to "win" an argument. Winning may bring momentary satisfaction but can leave lasting emotional scars. Winning the argument can mean losing the relationship. Prioritize harmony over victory.

For complex issues, involving a trusted mediator can provide clarity and guidance. A neutral third party- whether a friend, family member, elders, or professional - can help bridge communication gaps.

Lastly, practice empathy, step into their shoes before you step into a conclusion.

Listening with understanding fosters compassion, creating stronger and more resilient relationships.

The Power of Forgiveness

Forgiveness is one of the most valuable gifts you can give yourself. Carrying anger or resentment only weighs you down; letting go frees your heart and mind to heal and grow. Each time you forgive, you shift a loss into a personal gain, reclaiming your peace and emotional balance.

Holding onto grudges is like carrying a heavy burden. The sooner you forgive, the lighter you feel, not just emotionally but physically too. Forgiveness is not about excusing someone's wrongs - it's about doing what's best for your own well being. Even when mistakes are grave and hard to overlook, ask yourself: what good does it do to stay bitter?

You may not be able to forget every painful memory that you might have gone through, but choosing to release the anger attached to them gives you emotional freedom. Forgiving doesn't mean erasing the past; it means refusing to let it control your present. When you forgive, you break free from invisible chains that bind you to pain, hurt and resentment.

Deciding whether to forgive is a true test of your inner strength. Forgiveness is not weakness - it's an incredible show of emotional resilience. Each time you forgive, you demonstrate your power to raise above negativity. People around you may not always voice it, but deep down, they respect and admire your ability to let go with grace.

Harnessing the power to forgive is crucial if you want healthy and lasting relationships. Start small when someone hurts you, pause, breathe, and tell yourself, "I choose peace over pain." Over time, you'll find it easier to move past disappointments. Each act of forgiveness polishes you into a better, wiser version of yourself. By forgiving, you silently contribute to a kinder and more understanding world. Everytime you let go off grudge, you are helping humanity become a little more compassionate - and life has a way of returning that goodness back to you in its own time.

CHAPTER 7

The Role of Gratitude and Appreciation

"Isn't it the little moments of gratitude that make relationships feel valued and cherished?"

"How often do we take love and sacrifices for granted instead of appreciating them with a thankful heart?"

Celebrating the small things for stronger bonds

Gratitude and appreciation are powerful tools that nurture relationships. By acknowledging the little things. We create a sense of belonging, security, and joy. Starting by noticing and vocalizing positive moments. Expressing gratitude daily - whether for a partner's kindness, a friend's support, or a colleague's effort, strengthens connection. Simple gestures like saying "thank you" or "I appreciate you" can leave lasting impressions.

Spending meaningful time together builds emotional closeness, take morning walks, savor sunrise moments, or simply enjoy a cup of tea together. Nature offers a calm environment to connect - listen to bird song, admire blooming flowers, or feel the breeze against your skin.

Celebrate achievements, no matter how small. Applaud your partner's effort, be it a deliciously cooked meal, a new outfit, or a task well done. Complements fuel self-esteem and mutual respect. Creating shared experiences deepens bonds. Laughing over jokes, playing games, or enjoying a surprise dinner date deepens ties.

How Appreciation Strengthens Love

Expressing gratitude is a powerful way to deepen relationships. Appreciation has the ability to motivate, uplift and strengthen emotional bonds. When people feel valued, they are encouraged to continue their positive behavior, fostering mutual respect and trust.

To effectively show appreciation, start by acknowledging the efforts and qualities of those around you. Use kind words to express how thankful you are. For example, saying "I really admire how thoughtful you were when you helped me today" or "Your kindness made my day better," can leave a lasting impact.

It's essential to recognize these moments rather than allowing good deeds to go unnoticed. Overlooking positive actions can hurt feelings and demotivate people.

Remember, everyone - whether a child or an adult - carves appreciation. Kind words generate positive energy and create a nurturing environment.

However, consistency is key. Regular appreciation shows sincerity, while infrequent or exaggerated praise may feel insincere. Be genuine in your words, ensuring your gratitude reflects true feelings.

Creating Rituals of Gratitude

Creating rituals of gratitude goes beyond occasional thank-yous, it involves weaving appreciation into the fabric of daily life. One simple yet powerful practice is starting or ending the day with a gratitude journal. Jotting down a few things you are thankful for each morning helps frame your mindset positively. In the evening, reflecting on events that brought joy or support can shift focus from stress to appreciation.

Another effective ritual is expressing gratitude during shared meals. For instance before eating, each person can mention one thing they are grateful for that day. This not only fosters connection but also creates a culture of appreciation within families or teams.

In workplaces, managers can adopt a weekly "gratitude spotlights" where team members highlight other's contributions. Recognizing effort publicly not only uplifts individuals but also motivates the whole group.

Celebrating personal milestones - like birthdays or anniversaries - by writing notes of appreciation to loved ones can transform occasions into moments of deeper connection. These rituals may seem small but overtime, they strengthen bonds and create an environment where gratitude becomes a way of life.

Show your Appreciations through Actions

Simply expressing “thank you” is meaningful, but when paired with thoughtful actions, it becomes even more powerful. Acts of appreciation don’t need to be grand; sincerity is what makes them impactful. Consider writing a short note to a colleague who supported you during a difficult project. A handwritten message saying, “I saw how much effort you put in - thank you,” can mean more than formal recognition.

Helping someone without being asked - like bringing a cup of tea to a tired parent, offering to carry groceries for an elderly neighbour, or taking a chore your partner usually handles, shows you care through action. These gestures say, “I see you. You matter.”

Even in digital spaces, small actions go a long way. Sending a voice note to thank a friend, sharing a photo that brings back a shared memory, or making time for a quick call can brighten someone’s day.

In classrooms, teachers can leave a sticky note of encouragement on a student’s desk.

In friendships, remembering important dates and checking in without a reason strengthen bonds.

When appreciation is demonstrated regularly and intentionally, it nurtures trust, deepens connections, and reminds people they are valued - not just in words but meaningful ways.

Acknowledge Sacrifices

People often make quiet sacrifices that often go unnoticed - staying up late to help, adjusting plans, or giving up personal comfort for the good of others. Acknowledging these acts fosters mutual respect and emotional safety. A simple sentence like - "I know you gave up your time for this - I truly appreciate you," validates the other person's effort. Publicly recognizing sacrifices, when appropriate, can also uplift morale. Even small gestures, like bringing someone's favourite snack after a hard day or letting them sleep in - deserve acknowledgment. Over time, recognizing sacrifices cultivates a culture of gratitude. It tells others, "Your effort isn't taken for granted." When people feel seen and valued for what they give up, they are more likely to feel connected and supported.

Engage Through Active Listening

Listening attentively is a powerful way to express gratitude. By nodding your head, making affirming sounds like "okay," "mmh," or "I see," you signal that their words matter. These small but meaningful responses convey respect and appreciation, reinforcing that their presence and thoughts are valued.

To make this practice actionable, avoid distractions - put down your phone, maintain eye contact, and show openness through your body language. When a friend shares something personal, repeat a part of what they said to show you're turned in: "It sounds like you felt really overwhelmed after that meeting." This validates their feelings.

In group settings, active listening means giving others a chance to speak without interrupting, summarizing their points when needed, and asking follow up questions that show genuine curiosity. Whether in a workplace meeting or a family discussion, these actions foster trust and cooperation. Listening deeply isn't passive - it's a conscious choice to prioritize others.

True Gratitude Brings Satisfaction

When people feel acknowledged and appreciated, they feel satisfied. By combining words with thoughtful actions, you create a deeper sense of fulfillment - not just for others, but for yourself as well.

True gratitude is deeply satisfying because it shifts your focus from what's missing to what's already meaningful in your life. For example, taking a few minutes each evening to write down a few things you're grateful for - like a warm cup of tea, a kind colleague, or a peaceful walk - can rewire your mindset toward positivity. It's a habit proven to increase emotional resilience and long-term happiness.

Expressing sincere thanks to a teacher who helped shape your path, or revisiting a place from childhood to reflect on how far you've come, can evoke a deep emotional reward.

These acts anchor gratitude in real life experiences.

Even saying "thank you" to yourself after completing a tough task can instill a sense of internal satisfaction. Gratitude turns ordinary life into a series of meaningful moments, creating emotional wealth no money can buy.

CHAPTER 8

Building Trust in Long Distance and Digital Connections

"Can trust truly thrive in long-distance and digital relationships without consistency and open communication?"

"Isn't it important to balance virtual interactions with real emotional depth to keep connections strong?"

Maintaining Connections Across Distance

Building trust in long distance and digital connections requires effort from both parties. Effective communication is important, but balance is crucial. While regular contact is important, excessive calls or constant messaging can feel overwhelming. A reasonable approach, such as a daily call, or two, often works best.

Be sincere and honest about your activities, where you are, and what you've been doing. Sharing these details naturally builds trust. Avoid being overly inquisitive or suspicious, as they can create tension rather than closeness. Express how much you miss and value the other person - it's a powerful way to maintain emotional connection. When checking in, avoid focusing on only one person's well-being. Be general in your inquiries by asking about family, work, or mutual friends as well. This shows you genuinely care about their life as a whole and helps maintain balance in conversations.

Scheduling calls at a convenient time can make interaction more consistent and meaningful. Don't disappear without explanation and then reappear suddenly; inconsistency breeds doubt. While video calls are an excellent way to feel closer. Don't insist on them often, as they may feel intrusive. When busy, communicate openly instead of ignoring calls or messaging. A simple explanation like, "I am swamped today, but I'll be up with you tomorrow," keep expectations clear and avoid misunderstandings.

Sharing small details about your day or your plans tomorrow can foster closeness. Texting, while different from verbal communication, is an intimate and effective way to express feelings. Both methods have their strengths, and using a mix of them helps maintain warmth and connection.

Ultimately, trust thrives on honesty, consistency, and thoughtful communication. With mutual effort, long distance connections can become even stronger and more meaningful.

Overcoming Jealousy and Insecurity

Jealousy and insecurity are the natural emotions, especially in relationships where physical distance can heighten uncertainty. However, these feelings must be managed to prevent them from damaging your connection.

Trust is the foundation of any strong relationship, particularly in long-distance or digital connections. Building these trust requires being reliable, keeping your promises and being consistent in your words and actions. Establishing constant communication also plays a vital role ; regular, open conversations help bridge the emotional gap that distance can create. Equally important is having faith in your relationship. Choosing to believe in your relationship and choosing to believe in your partner's commitment can reduce unnecessary doubts. When insecurities arise, pause and reflect - often, they stem from personal assumptions rather than your partner's behavior. Practicing self-control and patience is essential, especially when your thoughts are influenced by unfounded fears.

If your partner has a troubled past that triggers your insecurities, it's understandable to feel concerned. However, dwelling excessively on past mistakes can overshadow the progress you've both made. Focus on the present and nurture what you are building together.

Trust thrives on understanding, patience and conscious effort. By focussing on growth rather than fear, you empower your relationship to flourish despite distance.

Digital Etiquette for Lasting Bonds

In the digital age, building and maintaining trust in long-distance relationships require thoughtful communication and mutual respect. While technology offers convenience, it's essential to nurture connections with care and consideration. Be mindful of your partner's privacy. Avoid being overly inquisitive or obsessive. Trust flourishes when individuals feel their space is respected. Regular check-ins are important, but excessive messaging may feel suffocating. Instead, focus on meaningful interactions.

Practice intentional communication by replying to important messages promptly and with genuine attention. Set mutual boundaries around texting or calling times to prevent unintentional pressure. Use technology positively, send encouraging notes, share updates thoughtfully, and respect "offline" mode from the other end without demanding instant responses. Always re- read your messages before sending to check for unintended tones that may sound harsh or dismissive; Be deliberate in creating safe, judgment free digital spaces where both of you can share openly without fear. Healthy digital habits foster lasting emotional bonds.

Celebrate Special Moments

A thoughtful message on a birthday, anniversary, or other significant day can make a lasting impression. Surprise gestures, like sending a heartfelt letter or a thoughtful gift, show you value the relationship.

In addition to remembering major milestones, take time to celebrate small wins and everyday moments - like completing a project, overcoming a tough week, or simply appreciating each other's presence. Set reminders for special dates if needed, so nothing important is missed. Personalized touches make a difference: send a voice note instead of a text, mail a handwritten card, or surprise them with a playlist curated just for them.

If distance allows, plan a virtual meal or organize a surprise video call with close friends or family. Thoughtful gestures don't always have to be grand : even a few sincere lines expressing pride, gratitude, or love can create emotional closeness. Consistently showing you remember and honour the little things builds a foundation of appreciation, loyalty, and deep trust over time.

Understand the Limits of Digital Communications

Texts, emails, or video calls lack the emotional depth of face-to-face interactions. Choose clear and precise language to avoid ambiguity. Misunderstandings often arise from vague or poorly worded messages, so make your intentions clear.

Whenever possible, match the communication tool to the importance of the message. Use a video calls for serious conversations or emotional discussions where facial expressions and tone matter. Avoid having sensitive discussions through short text that can easily be misinterpreted. Take the time to pause and think before replying, especially if emotions are running high. If a message feels unclear, ask for clarification instead of assuming. Use voice notes when nuance is important, and don't rely solely on emojis to convey complex feelings.

Also, be aware of the timing of the messages : late-night or early-morning messages may create unnecessary stress. When something feels too complicated to explain over text, suggest scheduling a call. Prioritizing clarity, patience, and tone in digital conversations helps protect trust and prevents unnecessary conflicts.

Be Consistent in your Behavior

Don't act in unpredictable ways. Maintain the way you normally communicate - whether warm, casual, or formal - so the other person knows what to expect. If you are feeling too tired, unwell, or having a bad day, communicate this honestly rather than suddenly withdrawing.

Consistency builds emotional security. Aim to keep your tone, style, and timing of communication steady. For example, if you usually send a "good morning" or "good night" message, missing it suddenly without explanation may cause unnecessary worry. If your routine needs to change, give a simple heads-up.

When plans shift, inform the other person promptly instead of disappearing. Small updates, like saying "I'll call back later today" or "Busy evening ahead, but thinking of you," help maintain connection without creating confusion.

Avoid swinging between over-communication and complete silence. Instead, maintain a natural rhythm that fits both your lives. If you need more personal space temporarily, express it kindly, reassuring the other person that the relationship remains important. Consistency isn't about rigid patterns: it's about reliable emotional presence. Being predictably caring and honest, even on difficult days, strengthens trust and reassures your partner of your commitment.

Balance your Two-way Communication

Avoid abrupt changes like disappearing mid-conversation, or repeatedly switching between online and offline modes. Frequent status changes such as busy, silent, or offline may confuse the other person. Consistency builds trust; unpredictable behavior weakens it.

To build a healthy communication rhythm, observe how your partner responds - do they prefer morning check-ins or evening reflections? Adapt your communication patterns to suit both schedules. Don't let one person carry all the weight of starting conversations. A simple message like, "Thinking of you - how's your day going?" can invite deeper connection without demanding too much.

If one person is always the listener or always the talker, imbalance grows.Share stories, ask open-ended questions, and give space for replies. For example, say, "Tell me more about your project - i'd love to hear how it's going," rather than simply replying with "Nice." When there's silence, don't jump to conclusions. Instead, check in with, "You've been quiet lately - is everything okay?"

Balanced communication shows that both voices matter and helps create a relationship where both people feel equally heard and valued.

Embrace Moderation

Frequent messages may overwhelm the other person, while too little may create distance. Strike a healthy balance by being present without being too intrusive.

Moderation is key to maintaining a relationship that feels safe, respectful, and sustainable. Instead of flooding your partner with constant updates or expectations for immediate replies, focus on meaningful, timely communication. Ask yourself, "Is this something that can wait, or does it truly need to be shared now?" This helps reduce pressure and keeps the conversation intentional.

Set gentle boundaries together. For instance, you might agree to take a short break from texting during work hours or social events, then catch up meaningfully later. Respect each other's routines and downtimes.

By practicing moderation, you show that you care about the other person's mental space while still staying connected. It reinforces trust, encourages mindful interaction, and allows the relationship to breathe and grow without feeling forced.

Use Emojis Appropriately

Emojis can add warmth and clarity to your words, but overusing them may dilute your message. A well-placed emoji can soften serious conversation or add playfulness to serious chats.

Be intentional when you use emojis. Instead of sending a string of icons, choose ones that reflect your tone or clarify your intent. For, example, if you're joking, a wink or laughing emoji helps avoid misinterpretation. If you are expressing care, a heart or smile can convey without needing long explanations.

However, avoid replacing words entirely with emojis especially during serious conversations. If your partner is upset or confused, emojis won't replace thoughtful words or understanding.

If unsure, observe how the other person uses emojis. Mirror their comfort level subtly. Ask directly if needed: "Do emojis help or confuse you when we chat?' That small question shows thoughtfulness.

Used wisely, emojis can enhance connection, Used poorly, they may create misunderstandings. Balance creativity with clarity for meaningful digital communication.

CHAPTER 9

Resilience In Relationships

"Isn't it the toughest storms that reveal the true strength of a relationship?

How can a bond grow deeper if it is never tested by life's challenges?"

Weathering Storms Together

Relationships are like the open sea - calm and beautiful at times, yet capable of turning stormy without warning. How you respond to these challenging moments determines whether you drift apart or emerge stronger together. Resilience requires patience, understanding and effort from both partners.

Conflict in relationships often stem from two sources: internal disagreements between partners and external pressures such as financial struggles, family interference, or social expectations. Regardless of the cause, both individuals must take responsibility in overcoming the challenge. Be the one to reach out and break the ice. Waiting for the other person to make the first move often prolongs the tension.

Imagine a couple stranded at the sea during a storm. They can either panic and risk cap sizing, or work together to stabilize their boat. The same applies to relationships where staying calm is essential. Emotional outbursts often worsen the situation, while patience allows clearer thinking. Communicate honestly to express your thoughts openly but calmly to avoid misunderstandings. Instead of focussing on who's right or wrong, focus on finding a solution that strengthens the relationship.

When facing difficulties, offering support is crucial. Sometimes just being present - without judgment or advice - can provide comfort. Encourage your partner by reminding them of their strengths and celebrating small victories together.

During tense moments, reflecting on how you first met can reignite emotional connection. Memories of shared laughter, milestones, or overcoming past challenges can remind you why you chose each other in the first place. Revisiting positive memories can soften conflict.

Understanding your partner's likes and dislikes also plays a vital role in maintaining harmony. Small gestures - like preparing their favourite meal or respecting their boundaries - can prevent unnecessary friction. Knowing what makes your partner happy shows care and thoughtfulness.

Resilient couples recognize that no one is perfect. Rather than fixating on flaws, they focus on the positive aspects of their relationship. Embracing imperfections with optimism strengthens your bond.

Above all, love is what holds everything together. Love nurtures patience, forgiveness and the willingness to stand by each other, even when things get tough. Love is the anchor that keeps your relationship steady through life's storms.

Just as every storm eventually passes, so do difficult moments in relationships. By reaching out, staying calm, and showing support, you can weather challenges and emerge with a deeper, more meaningful connection.

How Challenges Strengthen Bonds

Relationships are rarely free from difficulties, yet it is often through these very challenges that the strongest bonds are formed. When couples, friends, or family members face hardships together, they gain valuable insights that deepen their connection.

One of the most profound outcomes of overcoming challenges is a heightened sense of confidence, pride, and satisfaction. Facing adversity together cultivates resilience, allowing both individuals to see their combined strength. In these moments, we often develop a deeper attachment, built on shared experiences and a stronger emotional foundation.

Moreover, navigating through tough times encourages personal growth. As individuals, we gain self-respect by acknowledging our ability to ensure and adapt. This newfound strength often leads to improved boundaries, ensuring that each person's individuality and independence are maintained. Rather than feeling confined, partners or loved ones learn to respect one another's space, thoughts and emotions.

Challenges also offer an opportunity for reflection. We become less likely to repeat past mistakes after understanding what led to the difficulty in the first place. This self-awareness fosters better communication, improved decision-making, and greater trust. Interestingly, struggles can become a blessing in disguise, revealing hidden strengths. As we learn to navigate weaknesses, we rediscover qualities like patience, empathy, and perseverance,strengthening the bond we share.

Navigating Life Transitions as Team

Life is full of transitions, venturing out of your comfort zones and navigating these changes requires patience, understanding,and teamwork. Whether you're newly married, starting a family, or adjusting to retirement, embracing change together strengthens your bond.

For couples stepping into marriage, the journey begins with blending lifestyles, values, and routine. Establishing shared goals and maintaining open communication can ease this transition. It's important to embrace change as a team, recognizing that transitions are easier when faced together.

Starting a family introduces new responsibilities. From sleepless nights with infants to the excitement (and stress) of children studying school,college, and pursuing careers, these phases can feel overwhelming. During such times, couples should celebrate small wins to stay motivated and build positivity. Financial pressures may increase, requiring thoughtful budgeting and shared decision making to foster stability.

In some cases, couples may not decide to have children. While this path brings its own set of challenges, focussing on shared interests, building meaningful connections with others, and prioritizing personal growth can keep the relationship vibrant. Maintaining open communication to address concerns and expectations is crucial to ensuring both partners feel valued and understood.

Career demand can also bring changes. Job transfers or temporary separations may create emotional strain, but by maintaining regular communication, building trust and practicing a "two is better than one" mindset, couples can stay connected and strong despite the distance.

Retirement presents another major shift. After years of active work life, the sudden emptiness can feel unsettling. Couples can maintain purpose by exploring hobbies, volunteering in community activities, or even starting a new venture together. Embracing these activities helps maintain emotional well - being during uncertain phases.

Facing health challenges is another critical phase. Whether one partner experiences illness or both deal with age-related concerns, showing empathy, practicing patience and offering consistent care can significantly strengthen the relationship. Couples must also remember to prioritize self-care to support one another effectively.

Managing relationships with extended family can test resilience. Balancing in-law dynamics, caring for aging parents, or dealing with family conflicts requires setting healthy boundaries while maintaining compassion and respect.

Lastly, unexpected life events such as financial crises, natural disasters, or personal losses demand unity. Couples who face unexpected crises with calmness, and shared problem solving are better equipped to emerge stronger together.

By viewing transitions as opportunities for growth rather than obstacles, couples can build deeper trust, stronger connections and a resilient bond that withstands life uncertainties.

CHAPTER 10

Cultivating Lifelong Friendships

"Isn't true friendship built on trust, understanding and shared experiences over time?"

"How can a bond last a lifetime without effort, mutual respect, and genuine connection?"

Friendship is the foundation of strong and lasting relationships. Without this essential element, we risk taking our connections for granted - as if we own the other person. This sense of entitlement can strain both romantic and family ties.

In romantic relationships, friendship brings depth that goes beyond physical attraction or outward beauty. When two people share a bond of trust, respect, and genuine companionship, they create a relationship that withstands challenges. A relationship grounded in friendship nurtures open communication, shared values, and mutual support.

Similarly, in family dynamics, friendship can add warmth and joy. Between spouses, cultivating friendship helps maintain affection and understanding. Between parents and children, friendship can foster openness and trust. However, friendship in parenting must never override essential boundaries. While being approachable is important, parents must remain firm in setting rules and exercising authority. Failing to maintain this balance may blur roles, weakening parental guidance.

Cultural influences may shape how friendship is expressed within families. In some cultures parents maintain a clear hierarchical role, while in others, a more causal, friendship-driven approach is encouraged. Regardless of cultural norms, the key is to ensure that friendship complements - not replaces - the responsibilities of each role.

True friendship thrives on mutual respect, honesty, and healthy boundaries. By nurturing these qualities in romantic and family relationships, we create stronger, more meaningful connections that stand the test of time.

Building Deep Lasting Connections

Cultivating lifelong friendship requires nurturing the bond with thoughtful actions that keep the connection vibrant. Embracing routine with purpose is key - repeating kind gestures, shared activities, and meaningful conversations may seem ordinary, yet they are the foundation of lasting relationships. Consistency in doing good things should not be mistaken for dullness ; instead it's a quiet reminder that love and friendship thrive through steady care.

Creating memorable experiences can breathe new life into relationships. Plan occasional outings - whether it's a casual walk in the park, an overnight camping trip under the stars, or a relaxing day at the resort. Spontaneous surprises can also strengthen bonds - perhaps a handwritten note on a busy morning, a thoughtful gift for no reason, or a surprise coffee date after work.

Celebrating milestones, like birthdays and anniversaries, isn't just for children. Acknowledging special days keeps the spark alive, no matter how old you are. Even a simple candlelight dinner or a movie night can turn ordinary evenings into cherished memories.

Exploring new activities together can also deepen connections - try cooking a new recipe, starting a garden, or learning a craft side by side. Sharing creative moments encourages laughter and teamwork.

Above all, regular, meaningful conversations matter most amid life busyness. Set aside moments to talk - whether over a shared meal, during a quiet walk, or before going to sleep -instead of getting lost in your gadgets. In these moments of genuine connection, lifelong friendships find their roots, blossoming steadily through warmth, care, and shared joy.

Nurturing Old Friendships and Welcoming New Ones

Friendships are among life's greatest treasures, and nurturing them is essential for lasting connections. As the saying goes, "Old is Gold" - long standing friendships are precious because they have withstood the test of time. Cherish these relationships; they are not disposable commodities but living connections that enrich your life. Rather than neglect or discard old friends, preserve and nurture them, for they are rare gems that cannot be replaced.

Old friends shape us in profound ways. They have witnessed our growth, stood by us during struggles, and contributed to the person we are today. Recognizing this helps us appreciate their valuable role in our journey. Your wisdom today is, in part, a reflection of their influence.

While valuing old friendships, we must also remain open to new ones. Life is dynamic, and as we evolve, so should our social circles. Welcoming new friends expands our perspectives, introduces us to fresh ideas, and enhances our emotional well-being. Each person we encounter brings unique experience and insights. Embrace diversity and friendships ; every individual offers something to learn.

Moreover, cultivating new friendships demonstrates personal growth. Expanding your circle shows you are adaptable, curious, and open to change. The more meaningful connections you build, the richer and more fulfilling your life becomes.

In essence, lifelong friendships require conscious effort. Balance preserving old bonds with welcoming new ones, and you'll create a network of relationships that support, inspire, and uplift you throughout your journey. Friendships, when nurtured, become timeless treasures.

CHAPTER 11

The Power of Forgiveness and Letting Go

"Can a relationship truly move forward if the weight of past hurts is never released?"

"Isn't forgiveness more about freeing yourself than excusing the pain caused by others?"

Why Resentment Weaken Bonds

Relationship bonds are sensitive, delicate, and fragile - much like glass. Once broken, even if mended, the scars may remain. Holding on to resentment is like carrying a heavy burden ; it drains your emotional energy and strains your relationships.

When faced with conflict, it's crucial to focus on the present issue rather than dwelling on past mistakes. Constantly revisiting past grievances only strengthens resentment, making it harder to control.

Resentment, if unchecked, damages not only your relationship but also your well-being. While feeling resentful is normal, it's important to recognize its limits. Minor mistakes should be overlooked rather than met with harsh reactions. However, in cases of serious wrongdoing, expressing justified resentment can serve as a necessary signal that boundaries have been crossed. Ignoring such issues may embolden the other person to repeat harmful behavior.

The key lies in resolution and release. Once the issue is addressed, let go of lingering resentment. Harbouring unresolved bitterness keeps you shackled to negative emotions, preventing personal growth and space.

Resentment can quietly weaken the strongest bonds.- between friends, family members, and loved ones. Avoid adding fuel to the fire ; if you notice smoke, address it promptly, unresolved bitterness creates emotional distance, but forgiveness and letting go can restore trust, strengthen connections, and bring inner peace.

Healing from Hurt and Betrayal

It's natural to feel hurt when someone betrays your trust. The pain can be overwhelming, but dwelling on it won't change what has already happened. Acceptance is the first step towards healing - no matter how difficult it may be.

Don't isolate yourself. Negative thoughts thrive in solitude, making it harder to move forward. Instead, staying active helps break the cycle of negative thoughts - go out, connect with friends, engage in hobbies, or immerse yourself in meaningful activities. Distraction alone won't erase the pain, but it helps create space for positive emotions to take root.

Remember, this isn't the end of your journey. Every challenge teaches valuable lessons - one that strengthens your character and deepens your understanding of life.

Most importantly, love yourself. Remind yourself that you are worthy of happiness, respect, and peace. Loving yourself is crucial for emotional recovery. Self-acceptance builds resilience, allowing you to reclaim your inner strength.

Time is a powerful healer. While it may not erase the memories, it will soften the pain. If you believe a relationship is worth mending, approach it with honesty and courage. Giving second chances can be meaningful, especially when you've nurtured a relationship for years. Ending it abruptly may leave you with lasting regret. However, if reconciliation isn't possible, learn to let go. Both choices require strength, but trust that time will affirm your decision.

Ultimately, follow your inner voice. Healing isn't about ignoring the past; it's about freeing yourself from its hold. By choosing forgiveness - whether for yourself or others - you create space for peace, growth, and new beginning.

Finding Closure without Bitterness

Letting go is a powerful act that requires strength, patience, and a firm decision to move forward. When you decide to close a chapter in your life, embrace it fully - be decisive and firm. Dwelling on past issues after giving up only prolongs your pain. People respect those who stand by their decisions, especially in public matters. If you've made your choice, honor with confidence and accountability.

Words are powerful, and negative words can leave lasting scars. When faced with rumours, gossip, or misunderstandings, resist the urge to defend yourself at every turn. Have patience, silence often speaks louder than words. Over time, you'll realize that withholding unnecessary responses reinforces your seriousness and inner peace.

Be straightforward and honest in your interactions. Running from the truth only creates obstacles that can trap you later. Facing reality head-on may feel difficult at first, but it builds a stronger foundation for lasting closure.

If you are considering a new relationship, avoid acting in haste. Emotional wounds need time to heal, and rushing into new commitments can cloud your judgment. Relax and take a break; let time guide you naturally.

In family relationships, letting go may be less straightforward due to deep-rooted connections. While conflict may arise, biological ties often maintain a sense of responsibility and attachment. Parents, siblings, or close relatives may find it harder to sever relationships entirely. except in extreme cases.

Forgiveness doesn't mean forgetting - it's about releasing resentment and choosing peace over prolonged bitterness. By accepting what's beyond your control, you empower yourself to move forward with clarity, strength, and renewed purpose.

CHAPTER 12

Investing in Self-Growth for Healthier Relationships

"How can we build strong and healthy relationships if we neglect our own growth and well-being?"

"Isn't investing in self-improvement the first step toward deeper connections and lasting confidence?"

How Personal Growth Enhances Connection

Just as a child learns to communicate - moving from cries and gestures to words and meaningful conversations - adults too must actively develop skills to better themselves. Personal growth empowers us to express ourselves clearly, understand others, and build stronger relationships.

When individuals invest in self-growth, they develop greater self-awareness, emotional stability and improved social skills - all of which are vital for building healthy connections. By understanding their own emotions and thought patterns, people become better equipped to manage conflicts, offer empathy, and respond thoughtfully rather than react impulsively.

Emotional intelligence is key. Those who practice self-reflection, patience, and mindfulness are more attuned to the feelings of others. This fosters trust, respect, and deeper connections in personal and professional relationships.

Continuous Learning also Plays a Crucial Role

Continuous learning is not just an intellectual pursuit; it's a dynamic force that strengthens relationships. By committing to ongoing growth, individuals remain adaptable, open-minded, and receptive to change - qualities that are essential for maintaining healthy bonds. Learning new skills, whether communication techniques, conflict-resolution strategies, or emotional regulation practices, empowers individuals to navigate relational challenges with greater ease and understanding.

Practical continuous learning involves actively seeking feedback from trusted friends and partners, reading thoughtfully selected materials on emotional well-being, attending workshops that enhance interpersonal abilities, and intentionally stepping out of comfort zones to gain fresh perspectives. Regular self-evaluation - asking oneself questions like, "What can I do differently next time?" -keeps stagnation at bay.

Moreover, when individuals show a willingness to learn from mistakes, they cultivate humility and resilience - two pillars of strong, enduring relationships. Curiosity about others' experiences and viewpoints fosters deeper empathy, while embracing new methods of expressing care and appreciation revitalizes connection.

In essence, continuous learning is a conscious choice: it transforms relationships from static entities into evolving partnerships, enriched with authenticity, mutual growth, and renewed purpose.

Developing Self-Awareness

Developing self-awareness is essential for personal growth and building stronger relationships. Begin by closely analyzing yourself - what brings you joy, what irritates you, and what influences your emotional state. Observe where you feel happiest and most comfortable, and identify the people with whom you can truly be yourself. Pay attention to what makes you feel vulnerable, disappointed, or inspired.

Actively seek feedback from those around you. While not all feedback will be accurate, dismissing everything as false is unwise. Instead, reflect on the comments you receive. Ask yourself: Is there truth in this observation? If familiar feedback arises from different sources, take it seriously and explore ways to improve. Feedback is not always easy to accept, but embracing it can refine your character.

Develop the habit of reflecting on your actions. Examine what led you to behave in certain ways and what outcomes followed. Was your reaction driven by emotion, insecurity, or habit? Understanding your behavior patterns helps you make more intentional choices.

Surround yourself with honest, straightforward individuals who provide sincere, unbiased feedback. Their insights are invaluable for your self-improvement journey.

Step outside your comfort zone by exploring new experiences and environments. Doing so reveals how you respond to unfamiliar situations, exposing strengths you can build on and weaknesses you can address.

When receiving criticism, resist the urge to react defensively. Instead, consider their perspective thoughtfully. Negative feedback doesn't always mean you've failed - it may highlight areas you didn't notice before.

Building Confidence and Inner Peace

Personal growth and healthier relationships begin with a foundation of self-care. Prioritizing your physical,mental,and emotional well-being is crucial. When your body is well-nourished, your mind is clear, and your emotions are balanced, you naturally exude confidence.

To deepen this foundation, start by identifying the things that drain your energy or peace - then create boundaries around them. Schedule regular moments of stillness, such as early morning reflection or few minutes breathing breaks throughout the day. Journal your thoughts weekly to track emotional triggers and celebrate progress. Speak kindly to yourself - replace self-criticism with words of encouragement. Avoid comparing your life's journey to others ; focus instead on your personal growth goals. When you honour your values and keep your promises to yourself, you reinforce self-trust, an essential pillar of inner peace and authentic confidence.

Nourish Your Body and Mind

A healthy diet plays a significant role in boosting your self-confidence. Eating well, exercising regularly, and ensuring quality sleep contribute to your overall well-being. When you feel energetic and fit, you are better equipped to face challenges. Good health is the cornerstone of self-assurance.

To build on this, start with simple, mindful choices. Begin your day with lukewarm water and a nutritious breakfast. Plan your meals to include fresh fruits, vegetables, and whole grains that fuel both brain and body.

Minimize processed food that clouds your focus and slows you down. Commit to a few minutes of movement daily - whether it's a walk, dance, or stretching routine. If sleep is a struggle, establish a calming bedtime ritual; reduce screen time and engage in light reading or meditation. Also unplug briefly during the day - let your mind rest from overstimulation. Your mental clarity improves when your body is cared for consistently. Small daily efforts compound into strength and resilience.

Dress for Confidence

Your attire influences your self image. Dressing appropriately for different situations enhances your confidence and helps you feel prepared. Wearing clean, well-fitted clothes that reflect your personality can elevate your mood and improve your interactions. A thoughtful wardrobe reflects your self-respect.

To apply this practically, begin by understanding what clothing makes you feel most like yourself - comfortable yet presentable. You don't need to follow trends, but aim for neatness, good hygiene, and well-maintained outfits. Even working from home or stepping out briefly, dressing intentionally signals to your mind that you matter. Iron clothes, polish your shoes, and wear a scent that uplifts you. These small actions increase self-awareness and presence.

Additionally, choose colours that boost your mood - blue for calm, red for energy, or earthy tones for grounding. Keep a go-to outfit that never fails to boost your confidence on challenging days. Dress with the day's goals in mind ; preparing for a meeting? Go a level up in professionalism. Meeting a friend? Choose comfort blended with care.

The way you dress becomes part of your non-verbal communication, sending a clear message of how you value yourself - and others will mirror that respect back to you. However, there are exceptional occasions when your attire should reflect the significance of the moment rather than personal preference. Workplace dress codes may require formal or specific uniforms to maintain professionalism. Funerals call for respectful, subdued clothing as a sign of mourning and solidarity. Weddings often invite elegant or traditional attire to honour the couple's celebration.On cultural days or festivals, wearing garments that reflect heritage or community values shows respect for shared identity. These exceptions remind us that how we dress also expresses empathy, honour, and unity with others.

Sharpen Your Communication Skills

Effective communication is a powerful tool for building confidence. Knowing how to express your thoughts clearly in various situations empowers you to connect with others. Reading books, engaging in meaningful conversations, and practicing active listening are excellent ways to improve both your speaking and writing skills. Expanding your vocabulary sharpens your ability to articulate thoughts and ideas.

To build on this further, start by practicing clarity - avoid long-winded explanations and speak with purpose. Replace filler words like "um" or "you know" with thoughtful pauses. Use eye contact to build trust and reinforce engagement. Be mindful of tone - it shapes how your message is received.

Record yourself during practice conversations or presentations to identify areas of improvement. Ask for feedback from trusted friends or mentors. Learn to listen not just to reply, but to understand. This invites openness in your relationships.

Use journaling to process thoughts and emotions before expressing them aloud - it sharpens both internal clarity and verbal expression. Finally, remember: confident communication isn't about perfection but about authenticity. Speak honestly, stay calm under pressure, and be willing to go through feedback.

Every intentional conversation strengthens your confidence and deepens your relational impact.

Surround Yourself with Positive Influences

The company you keep has a significant impact on your mindset. Being around encouraging, supportive people nurtures your self-esteem. Positive social circles uplift you during challenging times and inspire you to become the best version of yourself. Positive connections foster confidence and inner peace.

To take this further, assess your current circle - do the people around you uplift or drain you? Make intentional choices to invest in relationships that encourage your growth. Attend interest-based groups, join learning communities, or volunteer - these environments attract people with shared positive values.

Set boundaries with negative or toxic individuals even if it feels uncomfortable at first. You don't have to cut ties harshly, but limit emotional exposure. Celebrate others' successes and share your challenges with those who show empathy.

Choosing to stay positive isn't something that just happens by chance - it's something you do on purpose. The people you spend time with should bring the kind of energy, respect, and encouragement that help you stay motivated and focussed.

Prioritize Mental and Emotional Balance

Taking care of your mental well-being is essential for achieving inner peace. Spend time in nature, practice mindfulness, and embrace moments of quiet reflection. Meditation, deep breathing, or simply disconnecting from daily stressors can refresh your mind and bring clarity. A calm mind is a confident mind.

To strengthen emotional balance, regularly check in with your feelings - journal your thoughts, speak to a trusted friend, or take short mental breaks during the day. Practice saying "no" without guilt when you are overwhelmed. Develop healthy coping mechanisms like walking, drawing or music instead of suppressing emotions. Emotional balance isn't avoiding feelings but understanding and managing them. With practice, you'll respond thoughtfully instead of reacting impulsively - bringing calm into your relationships.

Embrace Emotional Maturity

Emotional maturity means recognizing your emotions without letting them control your behavior. It starts with pausing before reacting - especially during disagreements. Practice staying calm when faced with criticism or frustration. Instead of blaming others, ask yourself what you can learn from the situation. Mature individuals listen to understand, not just to respond.

Respect boundaries, both yours and others'. Be willing to apologize when you are wrong, and forgive when needed - not to excuse, but to let go. Avoid passive-aggressive behavior; speak honestly and kindly. Emotional maturity also means showing up consistently - being reliable in actions, not just words. When you grow emotionally, you create space for safer, more respectful, and lasting connections.

Gratitude and Mindfulness

Gratitude and mindfulness are powerful habits that shift your attention from dissatisfaction to appreciation. Start by noticing the small things - a smile from a stranger, a moment of silence before a busy day, or the warmth of your morning drink. Write down a few things you are thankful for each night. This daily ritual rewires your brain to seek the positive.

Mindfulness is about being fully present. When talking to someone, listen without interrupting. Put your phone away during meals and pay attention to taste, texture, and smell. These tiny acts help anchor you in the now.

During stressful moments, pause and take a breath. Ask yourself: "What am I feeling? Why? That moment of reflection can stop reactive behavior and promote better decisions. Walk slowly outdoors, noticing trees, sounds, and the rhythm of your steps - let nature ground you.

Practice mindful gratitude when others support or encourage you. The more you recognize the good in your life, the more peace and joy you create within yourself and your relationships.

Practice Patience and Non-Judgment

In a fast-paced world, patience can feel like a forgotten virtue. Yet, cultivating it can bring calm to your interactions and clarity to your decisions. When someone speaks or acts in a way that irritates you, pause before reacting. Take a breath and ask yourself whether the issue is urgent or simply a matter of preference. Responding instead of reacting builds inner strength.

Non-judgment compliments patience. Instead of labelling people or situations as "good"or "bad" try observing without assigning meaning. When a friend cancels plans, rather than assuming carelessness, consider other possibilities. This open-mindedness reduces emotional friction.

Patience with yourself is vital keeping in mind that growth takes time. When progress feels slow, acknowledge the effort instead of the pace. Replace Your inner criticism with gentle encouragement. With time patience and non judgment become natural responses that foster trust, reduce conflict, and create a compassionate space - for yourself and others.

CHAPTER 13

Creating Shared Dreams and Goals

"Can a relationship truly thrive if both partners are moving in different directions?"

"Isn't the journey toward shared dreams more fulfilling when fuelled by mutual support and encouragement?"

Aligning Ambitions as Partners

In any relationship, whether personal or professional, aligning ambitions is crucial for shared growth and success. When two individuals come together, each with their own goals and dreams, the key is to find common ground and support each other's aspirations. This requires open communication, understanding and a willingness to adapt. Partners must discuss their ambitions openly, without fear of judgment, and create a space where both can thrive.

It's important to recognize that aligning ambitions doesn't mean sacrificing one's goal for the other. Instead, it's about finding ways to harmonize different dreams into a shared vision for the future. This alignment creates a sense of purpose and unity, providing the foundation for a strong, resilient partnership.

For example, one partner may have aspirations of advancing their career, while the other may dream of pursuing a creative passion. By discussing these ambitions and finding ways to balance time, energy, and resources, both partners can support each other in achieving their dreams without compromising their individual goals. Ultimately, aligning ambitions as partners is about mutual respect, encouragement, and the willingness to grow together, fostering a partnership where both individuals feel fulfilled and empowered.

Compromise Builds Stronger Connections

Relationships thrive on give and take. One practical way to build this balance is through scheduled check-ins where each partner can express what they need help with, be it time, support, or emotional flexibility. For instance if one partner is pursuing an advanced degree while the other manages a busy work schedule, both can agree to divide chores realistically without resentment. You can also use a shared calendar to align priorities, especially when individual commitment competes with relationship time. Making room for your partner's preferences in daily routines - like choosing movies, vacation spots, or even mealtime menus - signals that their happiness matters to you. Compromise isn't about sacrifice, it's about choosing connection over control. When both parties feel heard and are willing to adjust for other's well-being, compromise turns into a shared strength rather than a silent struggle. Over time, this mutual effort deepens understanding and strengthens the emotional foundation of the relationship.

Embrace Change

Change is inevitable - whether it's a career shift, relocation, health issue, or entering a new life phase. Facing these transitions as a united front rather than in isolation fosters a resilient relationship. Begin by creating a habit of change-readiness - embrace small changes regularly to normalize flexibility. For example, rotate household roles monthly or switch routines occasionally to develop adaptability. If your partner lands a job in a new city, focus on the potential growth it can bring rather than the discomfort of leaving familiarity.

It also helps to journal individual fears or expectations and then share them openly. This proactive sharing builds emotional safety and opens pathways for compromise. Celebrate small wins when navigating change - whether it's attending a new community event together or learning a new skill that benefits both. Make adaptability part of your relationship culture. Create a growth board together ; listing goals, dreams, and lessons learned through change.

Most importantly, support each other's evolving identities. What mattered to your partner five years ago may not hold the same weight now. Accepting and adjusting to each other's changing needs and roles keeps the relationships fresh, dynamic, and deeply rooted in mutual respect and vision.

Communication Nurtures Mutual Understanding

Strong relationships are built on open and consistent communication. This is more than just talking - it's about connecting. Schedule uninterrupted time weekly to check in emotionally, not just logistically. Ask questions beyond surface-level: "What's been on your mind lately?" or "How can I support you better this week?" These prompts invite deeper sharing.

Use tools like voice memos or handwritten notes when face-to-face talks are difficult. These personal touches convey care and attention. Learn each other's communication styles - some partners need space before discussing issues, others prefer immediate resolution. Respect those rhythms and don't assume silence means indifference.

Practice "mirroring" - repeat what your partner said in your own words to confirm understanding. For example: "So you felt ignored when I was on my phone during dinner, is that right?" This simple step can dissolve defensiveness and build empathy.

In moments of disagreement use the "pause and breathe" technique. Instead of reacting instantly, take a few seconds to breathe, then speak calmly. This creates space for thoughtful dialogue rather than emotional escalation.

When discussing sensitive topics, hold hands or sit side by side. Physical closeness can soften tension and promote unity. Lastly, celebrate good communication moments - thank your partner when they express themselves or listen patiently. This positive reinforcement encourages more of the same.

By nurturing honest, respectful communication, you lay the groundwork for a relationship that withstands misunderstandings, deepens emotional intimacy, and grows stronger over time.

Building a Vision for the Future Together

Building a meaningful relationship requires alignment in values, aspirations, and priorities. Achieving this begins with open communication without reservation - share your dreams and goals honestly, and encourage your partner to do the same. By being a patient listener, you gain deeper insight into their thoughts, fostering connection and trust.

Explore essential topics like personal interests, lifestyle preferences, and long-term ambitions. Discuss both short-term and long-term goals, from career growth to family planning and financial stability. Visualizing your relationship five to ten, or even twenty years ahead can help you create a shared vision for the future.

Set aside dedicated time for regular check-ins and progress reviews to ensure both of you are aligned and moving in the right direction. Flexibility is important since adapting to life's changes strengthens your partnership.

Above all, prioritize your relationship as a foundation of your shared journey. By investing in each other first, you build a solid base for future achievements.

Embrace compromise when differences arise, and focus on finding common ground. With intentionality, commitment, and consistent effort, you can create a fulfilling future built on mutual respect and collaboration.

The Role of Mutual Support in Achieving Goals

Mutual support plays a vital role in turning aspirations into reality. When partners collaborate they pool their strengths, ideas, and resources, enhancing both creativity and efficiency. By working together, individuals can achieve clarity, align strategies, and maintain motivation throughout the journey. The shared commitment not only accelerates progress but also strengthens the emotional bond between them.

Recognizing each other's strengths and limitations is crucial. Understanding where your partner excels allows you to delegate tasks wisely, while acknowledging your own shortcomings fosters humility and openness to learning. Combining diverse skills creates a well-rounded partnership, where one's weakness is balanced by the other's strength.

Mutual support also transforms obstacles into growth opportunities. Facing challenges together builds resilience, encouraging both partners to stay focussed and adaptable. Moreover, shared accountability fosters consistency, making it easier to stay committed to long-term goals.

Beyond practicality, working together can be enjoyable. Collaborative efforts often lead to moments of laughter, shared achievements, and deeper emotional connections. Adding professionalism to these dynamics ensures that personal bonds do not overshadow focus and productivity.

Ultimately, mutual support paves the way for successful outcomes in both work and relationships. By fostering trust, communication, and a shared vision, partners can achieve goals faster, with greater fulfillment and lasting connection.

CHAPTER 14

Love Across Generations

"How can we truly understand ourselves if we ignore the lessons and wisdom passed down through generations?"

"Isn't bridging the gap between past and present the key to preserving the values that shape our future?"

Learning from Family History and Traditions

Family traditions are more than just rituals; they are powerful tools for building stronger relationship bonds. By adapting these traditions to suit modern life, we can create meaningful connections that transcend generations.

Traditional societies offer valuable insights for younger generations. These communities are often close-knit, honest, and open-minded. Their simplicity, closeness to nature, and caring spirit reflect a deep understanding of human connection. Learning from such values can guide us in nurturing our own relationships. In addition to strengthening bonds, family traditions teach patience, mutual respect, and the importance of togetherness. They allow individuals to experience a sense of belonging, building trust that lasts beyond temporary challenges. These rituals, whether small daily customs or grand celebrations, act as anchors that provide security and comfort through life's uncertainties.

Moreover, they serve as a bridge between the past, present, and future, keeping family stories alive and preserving the essence of identity. Through such inherited practices, we not only cherish memories but also learn to appreciate sacrifices, dreams, and hope that shape who we are. As families adapt old customs to modern lifestyles, the heart of these traditions - love, unity and understanding - continues to thrive, making them timeless treasures for nurturing deeper relationships.

Connecting with our roots helps us rediscover the wisdom of our forefathers.

Their lifestyles and principles, rooted in authenticity, provide practical guidance for navigating life's challenges. By embracing these lessons, we gain strength during difficult times and find encouragement when life feels uncertain.

Connecting with our roots is not merely an emotional exercise; it's a journey into the foundation of who we are. Our ancestors, through their wisdom and lived experiences, offer blueprints for resilience, integrity and compassionate living. Understanding their ways of life deepens our sense of purpose and fosters gratitude to the struggles they overcame.

Every tradition, every value passed down, holds within lessons of perseverance, unity, and unconditional support.

When we reconnect with these roots, we learn to balance modern aspirations with timeless virtues. We realize that the courage to face adversity, the wisdom to choose kindness over anger, and the strength to uphold relationships even in times of difficulty, are not new challenges but ones our forefathers faced and conquered with dignity, Their insights into community living, respect for nature, and prioritization of family reveal profound truths applicable even today. As we rediscover these gems of wisdom, we find pathways to lead more meaningful lives, centered around empathy and purpose. In honouring their legacy, we empower ourselves to create a future where love, respect, and authenticity continue to guide human connection across all generations.

Our heritage is a treasure trove of wisdom.

Family memories are powerful reminders of love and care. Shared stories, cherished traditions, and cultural practices serve as a guidebook for fostering lasting bonds. These memories reinforce identity, offering comfort and direction when we face crossroads in life.

Our heritage is rich not only with traditions but also with life lessons crafted through generations of lived experiences. It carries the values of endurance, compassion, humility, and respect, offering practical wisdom that modern life sometimes overlooks. Heritage reminds us that life's most insignificant achievements often come from persistence, collaboration, and faith in one another.

As we explore the customs and practices of our ancestors, we uncover principles that offer timeless relevance: honouring commitments, valuing hard work, forgiving mistakes, and standing firm in truth. In times of uncertainty, drawing from this reservoir of collective wisdom provides both solace and strength. Every cultural ritual, every family story whispered through generations, adds a layer of resilience and hope to our character. Embracing our heritage means allowing its wisdom to inspire our choices, enriching our lives with meaning and direction. Thus, our heritage continues to be an everlasting wellspring, nurturing the spirit of love, unity and wisdom within us.

Bridging Generation Gaps in Values

Have you ever wondered why certain values, traditions, or beliefs seem so different across generations? While it's natural for each age group to develop its own way of thinking, the key to building meaningful relationships lies in embracing these differences rather than resisting them.

To connect across generations, we must start with an open mind. Be willing to explore and understand the values, beliefs, and traditions of older generations. Instead of dismissing their ways as outdated, recognize that they are often grounded in wisdom shaped by experience. After all, isn't it remarkable how much we can learn from those who've lived through changing times?

When visiting new places or interacting with unfamiliar communities, take time to understand the local context - their language, lifestyle, and cultural practices. This helps build trust and shows respect.

One of the most powerful ways to connect is to listen more than you speak. Ask questions, be curious, and show genuine interest. Learning from others not only broadens your perspective but also reveals the richness of their experiences.

Be flexible in your thinking. Embracing different viewpoints doesn't mean losing your own - it means gaining insight and understanding.

Connecting with younger generations also requires thoughtful effort:

Embrace technology - Younger people often express themselves through digital platforms. Engaging with these tools can strengthen your bond.

Show respect for their ideas - Even if their thoughts seem unconventional, showing interest encourages meaningful dialogue.

Join in their activities - Whether it's sports, music, or creative hobbies, participating shows that you value their world.

Lastly, don't isolate yourself even as you age, try to engage with people of all ages. The wisdom of elders is a treasure trove of knowledge, while the energy and ideas of youth offer fresh perspectives. By combining these approaches, you'll foster stronger connections across generations, enriching your understanding of life itself.

Preserving Wisdom While Embracing Change

Love is universal, transcending time and generations. But how do we preserve the wisdom of the past while embracing the changes that shape our future? The answer lies in finding balance - a blend of honoring tradition and welcoming innovation.

Passing down your wisdom is not just an act of teaching; it is an act of love - a gift that enriches those who come after you. When you share life lessons, memories, and values, you offer guidance that empowers the next generation. Yet, in doing so, it's vital to remember that change is inevitable.

How can we stay rooted in timeless values while adapting to modern realities? The key is to remain steadfast in principles like integrity, respect, and compassion, yet flexible enough to accept new ideas. Embracing change does not mean abandoning the past ; it means building on it with wisdom and purpose.

Life is a continuous learning process. Are you willing to step out of your comfort zone to discover new possibilities? Openness to learning ensures growth, while clinging too tightly to outdated ways may limit progress. Change may feel unsettling at first, but consider it not as a disruption - but as the new normal.

Navigating life's transition requires resilience and courage. Embrace uncertainties with confidence and renewed strength. Rather than resisting change, ask yourself: What can this teach me? How can this enhance my understanding of the world?

Preserving wisdom is not about dwelling in the past but about carrying its light forward. By blending the richness of tradition with the freshness of new ideas, you can create a legacy of love that transcends generations - a legacy that inspires, nurtures, and endures.

CHAPTER 15

Everlasting Power of Love

"Isn't true love more than just a feeling,but a daily choice to stay committed and grow together?"

"How can love leave a lasting legacy if it isn't nurtured with care, patience, and devotion?"

Understanding Love as a Choice and Commitment

Love is not a fleeting emotion or a passing attraction - it is a conscious choice and a deliberate commitment. When you choose a friend, a partner, or even someone to trust deeply, you are not selecting something temporary like a fashion trend or a gadget. You are choosing a human heart and soul - something far more precious and fragile.

So, how do you make the choice wisely? Ask yourself: Am I prepared for the responsibility that love demands? True love isn't about excitement alone; it requires patience; understanding, and sacrifice. Are you ready to invest your time, emotions, and energy to nurture this bond? Love doesn't grow effortlessly; like a seed, it must be watered with sincerity, hard work, and obedience to the values that sustain it.

Before making your choice, consider. Have I prepared myself for this commitment? Love is not about trial and error; it's about making a thoughtful decision and standing by it. When you commit to someone, you are not only accepting their strengths but also embracing their flaws.

True Love Preserves, even when Challenges Arise.

It's easy to be swept away by feelings in the moment, but ask yourself: Am I prepared to love even when the feelings fade? Feelings fluctuate, but commitment holds strong when emotions waver. That's why taking time to choose is essential. Rushing into relationships without reflection often leads to regret.

Once you've made your choice, don't turn back at the first sign of difficulty. Instead, stand firm, remembering that love's greatest power lies in its ability to ensure. Choosing to love is choosing to stay. Even when the road feels uncertain.

Keeping Romance Alive Over Time

Love isn't only about the grand moments; it's about the small, everyday choices that keep the connection strong. So, how can you ensure your love stands the test of time? First, build a habit of celebrating the ordinary. Do you praise your partner for everyday efforts - like making a cup of tea, fixing a lightbulb, or simply being there? Gratitude turns routine into romance.

Next, embrace shared curiosity. Have you explored a hobby together recently? Whether it's cooking a new recipe, learning a dance move, or even hiking a new trail, discovering new experiences side by side can reignite excitement.

What about laughter? Couples who laugh together stay connected. Try inside jokes, funny memories, or even harmless teasing to keep things lighthearted.

Don't forget the power of unexpected surprises. A spontaneous breakfast in bed, an impromptu picnic, or a sudden weekend getaway can speak volumes. Isn't love strongest when it feels spontaneous?

Equally important is creating a safe space for emotional vulnerability. When was the last time you sat quietly, sharing your fears, dreams, and thoughts without judgment? Emotional closeness builds lasting trust.

Another powerful tool is embracing shared rituals. Creating meaningful traditions - whether it's a Sunday morning coffee date, an evening walk, or a monthly "memory night" where you revisit all photos or letters - can deepen your bond. Isn't love nurtured best when woven into the fabric of daily life? These rituals provide stability while reminding you both of the moments that brought you together in the first place.

Finally, make room for individual growth. Encourage each other's personal goals, and celebrate milestones - big or small. Love flourishes when both partners thrive as individuals.

Love as a Legacy

Love is more than just a fleeting emotion; it's a force that shapes our very existence. From the moment we are born, love surrounds us - nurturing us as children, guiding us as adults, and comforting us in our later years. It's not confined to a single chapter of life; rather, it returns to us again and again, reminding us of its enduring power.

But where does this love come from? Is it merely a feeling we stumble upon - or is it something far deeper - a legacy inherited through generations. What if love is the most priceless inheritance we can ever pass on?

We learn to love from our parents - through their warmth, their sacrifices, and their unwavering presence. As we grow, love takes new forms: the laughter of friends, the kindness of neighbors, the support of colleagues and the unspoken bond within our local community. Each experience shapes us, planting seeds that will blossom in the lives of those we encounter. Love is the cornerstone of every meaningful relationship - binding families, strengthening friendships, and fostering unity in communities.

Without love, trust withers, understanding fades, and connections break apart. It is love that breathes life into our bonds, turning simple association into lasting relationships.

Yet love is not self-sustaining, it requires care, attention self-sustaining. What happens when we fail to nurture it? What if we forget to pass it on. Keeping the flame of love burning is a responsibility we all share.

By choosing kindness over indifference, forgiveness over resentment, and compassion over judgment, we ensure that love outlives us thriving in the hearts of future generations.

Have you ever considered how even the smallest act of love can ripple over time? A word of encouragement, a moment of patience, or a gentle smile may seem insignificant, yet these gestures can leave lasting imprints.

We must do more than experience love; we must cultivate it, cherish it, and pass it on - stronger, deeper, and richer than what we inherited. For love, when given freely and abundantly, becomes an external flame - one that no darkness can extinguish.

Living the Golden Rules Everyday

Choosing Love, Trust, and Connection as a Lifestyle

Can you imagine a life without love? A life without warmth, without someone to share your joys and sorrows? Love is the heartbeat of our existence. It fills our lives with meaning, comfort, and purpose.

But what is love without trust? Can true love survive without trust? Trust is the foundation that holds relationships together. Without it, doubt creeps in, and love starts to wither. Trust strengthens bonds, deepens connections, and creates a sense of security that allows love to flourish.

Now imagine living without connection. No conversations with family, no laughter with friends, no shared moments with colleagues - life would feel empty and isolated. We are wired to connect ; it's how we grow, learn, and find fulfillment. Connection makes us whole.

Our happiness, our sense of purpose, and even our hope are deeply tied to love, trust, and meaningful connections. So why not make these values a part of your daily life? Greet a stranger with a smile, call a loved one just to say Hello, or extend a hand to someone in need.

Love, trust, and connection aren't just emotions - they are choices. Choose them every day, and you'll find your life richer, happier, and more fulfilling.

Embracing Imperfection

To err is human. None of us are perfect, and that is a truth we must accept. But how often do we truly embrace this reality in our daily lives? Do we have the courage to admit our mistakes openly and honestly?

Admitting our mistakes requires bravery. It takes strength to acknowledge when we've gone wrong, especially when pride tempts us to hide our flaws. Ignoring our imperfections only creates deeper problems. In fact failing to admit mistakes reveals one's weakness, not strength. Isn't it far more courageous to own up our errors than to pretend they never happened?

Equally important is our attitude towards the mistakes of others. Just as we are imperfect, so are those around us. Understanding this helps us develop empathy and patience. How can we expect forgiveness if we are unwilling to extend it to others?

To live the golden rules everyday, we must make conscious efforts to embrace imperfection. Do we take time to reflect on our actions each day? Starting your day with self-reflection can help you recognize areas where you may have fallen short. Apologising promptly when you realize you've hurt someone shows responsibility and courage. Practicing patience reminds us that others are navigating their own struggles too.

Recognizing our own shortcomings is the first step to understanding those of others. Without this awareness, we risk becoming overly critical, blind to our own faults. Embracing our flaws - and allowing space for others to do the same - fosters humility.

Every day, knowingly or unknowingly, we stumble. But instead of dwelling on guilt or blame we should see these moments as opportunities to grow. Admitting our mistakes with courage, learning from them with humility, and extending grace to others is a golden rule we must carry with us. Wouldn't the world be a kinder place if we all lived by these principles?

Committing to Growth in Relationships

Dedication and consistency are vital for sustaining a meaningful relationship. While love may ignite the spark, it's the ongoing effort that keeps the flame burning. Growth in relationships doesn't happen overnight - it's a gradual process that requires patience, understanding, and attention.

What happens when you stop nurturing your relationship?

Without consistent effort, relationships risk becoming stagnant, monotonous, and uninspired. A relationship that lacks growth often feels lifeless - like a stream with no movement. To keep it vibrant, both partners must actively contribute to its progress.

How can you ensure your relationship continues to grow?

***Prioritize Communication**: Regular, open conversations foster deeper understanding. Don't wait for conflicts to take roots; share your thoughts, dreams, and concerns consistently.

***Celebrate Small Wins**: Growth isn't always about big milestones. Acknowledging small achievements - like overcoming a disagreement or supporting each other through challenges - strengthens your bond.

***Embrace Change Together**: Love evolves, and so should relationships. Be willing to adapt and explore new interests or ideas as a couple.

***Be Intentional with Time**: Don't leave meaningful moments to chance. Plan activities that allow you to connect and grow emotionally.

Are you taking your relationship for granted?

Complacency is one of the biggest threats to lasting connections. When you stop investing in your relationship, distance can quietly build. Consistency - in words, actions, and affection - is the antidote to stagnation.

By embracing these principles daily, your relationship can remain fresh, fulfilling, and full of life.

About the Author

Kerry Lots MA (English) B.Ed is a passionate English teacher.With over 10 years of experience in the field of education. He brings together his love for language, learning, and love to write about personal growth, relationships, and well - being.

Dedicated to moulding children and nurturing their potential Kerry Lots find deep fulfillment in guiding young minds both academically and personally.

Deeply interested in culture and tradition, he weaves these themes into his work to preserve values and spark meaningful reaction.

As an author Kerry aims to inspire and empower readers through relatable stories and practical wisdom drawn from both classroom and personal journey.

While he is not teaching he enjoys poetry,music, cooking, and appreciates the calming beauty of nature.

With over a decade of experience teaching English, Kerry believes in the power of words to educate, inspire, and transform lives.

Kerry loves to write poems on nature, spending time with children, finding joy and inspiration in their curiosity and innocence. When not writing, Kerry loves to spend time with family, reading books, listening to music, gardening and appreciating the beauty of nature.

www.ingramcontent.com/pod-product-compliance
Lightning Source LLC
Chambersburg PA
CBHW062142160726
48282CB00027B/916